W9-ARJ-715

MEXICO

EXPLORE THE COUNTRIES · EXPLORE THE COUNTRIES · EXPLORE THE COUNTRIES · EXPLORE THE COUNTRIES

Sarah Tieck

Big Buddy **BOOKS**
Explore the
Countries

VISIT US AT

www.abdopublishing.com

Published by ABDO Publishing Company, PO Box 398166, Minneapolis, MN 55439.

Copyright © 2014 by Abdo Consulting Group, Inc. International copyrights reserved in all countries. No part of this book may be reproduced in any form without written permission from the publisher. Big Buddy Books™ is a trademark and logo of ABDO Publishing Company.

Printed in the United States of America, North Mankato, Minnesota.
042013
112013

♻ PRINTED ON RECYCLED PAPER

Coordinating Series Editor: Rochelle Baltzer
Contributing Editors: Megan M. Gunderson, Marcia Zappa
Graphic Design: Adam Craven
Cover Photograph: *Shutterstock*: holbox.
Interior Photographs/Illustrations: *Alamy*: © Aurora Photos (p. 35), © Everett Collection Historical (p. 11), © Photocuisine (p. 27); *AP Photo*: AP Photo (p. 31), Julio Cortez (p. 29), GDA via AP images (pp. 29, 33), Dario Lopez-Mills (p. 19); *Getty Images*: Mary Ann Anderson/MCT via Getty Images (p. 17), DEA/G. DAGLI ORTI (p. 15), Susana Gonzalez/Bloomberg via Getty Images (p. 25); *Glow Images*: Helmut Corneli (p. 23), H. Tom Hall/National Geographic Image Collection (p. 16), Christian Kober (p. 21); *iStockphoto*: ©iStockphoto.com/abalcazar (pp. 9, 38), ©iStockphoto.com/cristianl (p. 35), ©iStockphoto.com/YinYang (p. 35); *Shutterstock*: alexsvirid (p. 13), ChameleonsEye (p. 34), Globe Turner (pp. 19, 38), NCG (pp. 9, 11), Ronald Sumners (p. 37), VICTOR TORRES (p. 34), Joao Virissimo (p. 5).

Country population and area figures taken from the CIA World Factbook.

Library of Congress Control Number: 2013932151

Cataloging-in-Publication Data

Tieck, Sarah.
  Mexico / Sarah Tieck.
    p. cm. -- (Explore the countries)
  ISBN 978-1-61783-816-3 (lib. bdg.)
  1. Mexico--Juvenile literature.   I. Title.
  972--dc23
                                                              2013932151

MEXICO

Contents

AROUND THE WORLD

Our world has many countries. Each country has beautiful land. It has its own rich history. And, the people have their own languages and ways of life.

Mexico is a country in North America. What do you know about Mexico? Let's learn more about this place and its story!

Did You Know?
Spanish is the official language of Mexico.

Mexico is famous for its beautiful beaches.

5

PASSPORT TO MEXICO

Mexico is located in the southern part of North America. Three countries border it. The Pacific Ocean, the Gulf of Mexico, and the Caribbean Sea also border Mexico.

Mexico's total area is 758,449 square miles (1,964,375 sq km). About 115 million people live there.

WHERE IN THE WORLD?

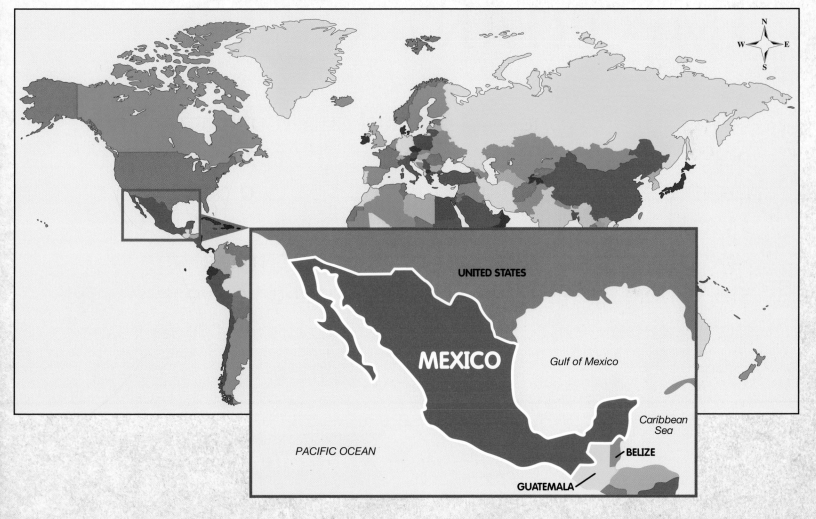

UNITED STATES

MEXICO

Gulf of Mexico

Caribbean Sea

PACIFIC OCEAN

BELIZE

GUATEMALA

IMPORTANT CITIES

Mexico City is Mexico's **capital** and largest city. It is home to about 8.9 million people. The city is a center for business, education, and the arts.

Mexico City has grown quickly because of business and government. Old-fashioned Spanish buildings stand next to modern buildings. Parts of the city are very poor. Some people do not have safe drinking water or electricity.

Did You Know?

Mexico City is the main city in a group of cities called a metropolitan area. About 20 million people live in this area.

A monument honors those who fought for Mexico's independence. It is on Paseo de la Reforma, which is a major street in Mexico City.

MEXICO

Guadalajara •
Mexico City ★ Ecatepec de Morelos

Plaza de la Constitución is in the center of downtown Mexico City.

Ecatepec de Morelos is Mexico's second-largest city. It has about 1.7 million people. It is part of the Mexico City **metropolitan** area. It was important during the Mexican fight for independence. Today, a museum honors the city's history.

Guadalajara is Mexico's third-largest city, with about 1.5 million people. It is in a rich farming area. It is also the **capital** of the state of Jalisco. Pottery and glass products are made there.

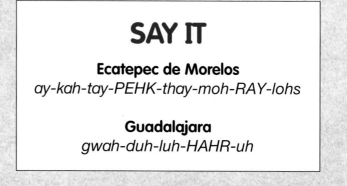

SAY IT

Ecatepec de Morelos
ay-kah-tay-PEHK-thay-moh-RAY-lohs

Guadalajara
gwah-duh-luh-HAHR-uh

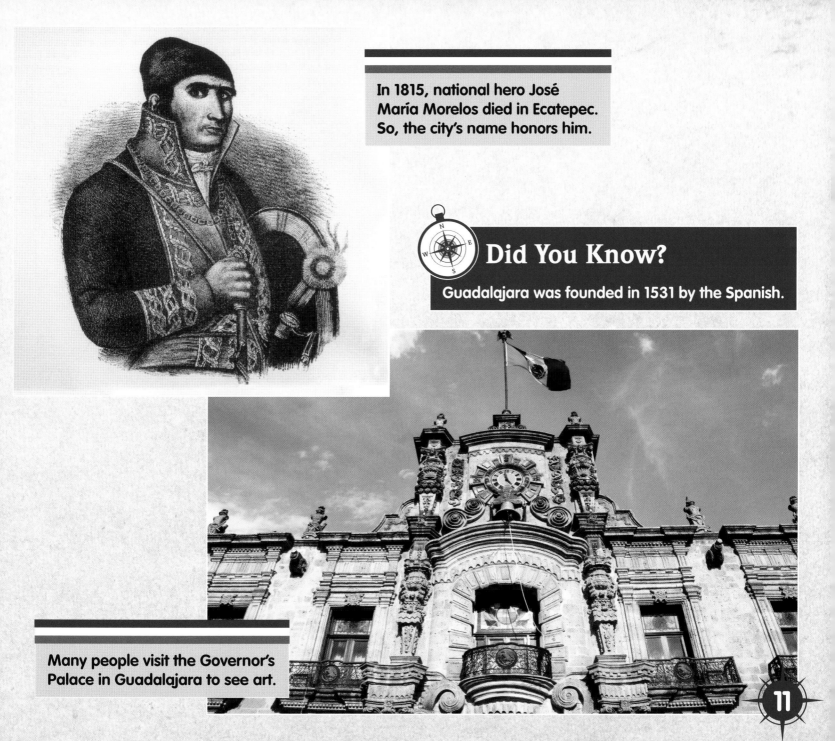

In 1815, national hero José María Morelos died in Ecatepec. So, the city's name honors him.

Did You Know?

Guadalajara was founded in 1531 by the Spanish.

Many people visit the Governor's Palace in Guadalajara to see art.

Mexico in History

The first people to live in Mexico were hunters. They arrived from the north earlier than 8000 BC while following animal herds. Later, people began farming and stayed in the area.

As people settled, villages grew. Over time, several great **civilizations** formed. The Maya held power between AD 250 and 900. They built pyramids.

Beginning in the 1300s, the Aztecs built the last great native civilization. They were **conquered** by the Spanish in the 1520s.

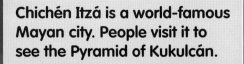

Chichén Itzá is a world-famous Mayan city. People visit it to see the Pyramid of Kukulcán.

13

Spain ruled Mexico for about 300 years. But, Mexicans did not want to be controlled by the Spanish. In 1821, Mexico won its freedom from Spain.

Mexico worked to become its own country. But, people fought with each other. And in the 1840s, Mexico and the United States fought over land.

The Mexican **Revolution** began in 1910. When it ended in 1920, the country had changed. Today, Mexico faces population growth and a lack of jobs. But, Mexicans are working to improve their country.

Did You Know?

Mexico honors Independence Day on September 16.

Agustín de Iturbide helped free Mexico in 1821 and became the country's ruler. People celebrated as he entered Mexico City.

Timeline

About AD 250

The Mayan people began to build cities and pyramids. They made art, calendars, and an advanced writing system.

About 1150 BC

The Olmec people began building their **civilization**. It was one of the first in North America. They made a calendar and a counting system.

About 1325

The Aztecs founded Tenochtitlán. This later became Mexico City.

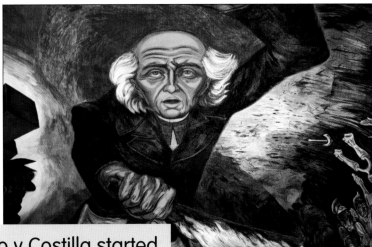

1810

Miguel Hidalgo y Costilla started Mexico's fight for independence.

1521

Hernán Cortés of Spain **conquered** the Aztecs.

2010

Mexico celebrated 200 years as an independent country.

An Important Symbol

Mexico's flag was first adopted in 1821. Today's version was adopted in 1968. It has three stripes. They are green, white, and red. An eagle and snake are in the center.

Mexico's government is a **federal republic**. There are 31 states and a federal district. Mexico's Congress makes laws. The president is the head of state and head of government. He or she is elected for one six-year term.

The eagle and snake in the center of Mexico's flag stands for an Aztec story. The Aztec built their capital where they saw an eagle eat a snake.

Mexico's president Enrique Peña Nieto took office in December 2012.

ACROSS THE LAND

Mexico has mountains, deserts, coasts, forests, and rain forests. Sierra Madre is a mountain system covering much of Mexico. A group of active **volcanoes** are in southern Mexico.

Mexico is bordered by the Pacific Ocean, the Gulf of Mexico, and the Caribbean Sea. The Rio Grande is in the north. This river forms about a 1,250-mile (2,010-km) border with the United States.

Pico de Orizaba is the country's highest point. It is about 18,410 feet (5,610 m) high.

Did You Know?

In May, the average temperature in Mexico City is 66°F (19°C). In December, it is 54°F (12°C).

Many types of animals make their homes in Mexico. These include lizards, coyotes, rattlesnakes, jaguars, and parrots. Fish and shellfish are found in the coastal waters.

Mexico's land is home to many different plants. These include pine and palm trees. Cacti are found in the deserts. Flowers such as orchids, poinsettias, and geraniums also grow in Mexico.

Did You Know?

Chihuahuas are the world's smallest dogs. They first came from Mexico.

Mexico's Caribbean coast has coral reefs filled with colorful fish.

Earning a Living

In Mexico, many people work in factories. The country's factories make cars, steel, food, and beverages. Other people have service jobs. They may work for the government, in schools, or helping visitors.

Mexico has important natural **resources**. Silver, gold, iron ore, and oil come from its land. Farmers produce crops including corn, avocados, and mangoes. They also raise beef and dairy cattle.

Many food products are made in Mexico City.

LIFE IN MEXICO

Many people in Mexico live in cities. These often have a mix of skyscrapers and historic buildings. People can visit museums and libraries. Mexico is known for its authors, artists, and musicians.

Foods in Mexico are often spicy and seasoned with hot peppers. Beans, or *frijoles*, are a common food. Corn tortillas are often served with meat, cheese, and beans. Avocados and mangoes are common fruits. Coffee, milk, and soda are favorite drinks.

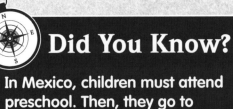

Did You Know?

In Mexico, children must attend preschool. Then, they go to school from ages 6 to 18.

Burritos are a popular dish in Mexico.

Mexicans enjoy sports. Football, or soccer, is a very popular sport. Baseball is another favorite. People go to games and many play on local teams.

Religion is important in Mexico. Most people are Roman Catholic. Many of the country's holidays are religious. Early people honored nature, ancestors, and other spirits in their religion. These beliefs are often combined with Roman Catholic **traditions**.

Guadalupe Day takes place on December 12. It honors a saint named Our Lady of Guadalupe.

Las Posadas takes place for nine days before Christmas. Each night, people act out Mary and Joseph's famous trip to Bethlehem. Then, children hit a piñata.

FAMOUS FACES

Mexico is known for art. Diego Rivera is a famous painter. He was born on December 8, 1886, in Guanajuato.

Rivera often painted large, colorful pictures called murals. He painted them on walls in public places. His murals shared his strong ideas about life in Mexico and the Mexican **Revolution**. He died in 1957.

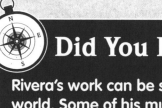

Did You Know?

Rivera's work can be seen around the world. Some of his murals are at the National Palace in Mexico City.

Rivera often painted frescoes. These types of paintings are done on wet plaster. The paint becomes part of the surface.

Diego Rivera was married to another famous Mexican painter. His wife Frida Kahlo was born on July 6, 1907, in Coyoacán.

At age 18, Kahlo was hurt in an accident. This caused health problems for the rest of her life. Like Rivera, she had strong ideas about life in Mexico. But, her colorful paintings were often about her feelings and her life. Kahlo died in 1954.

Did You Know?

Kahlo's house was called the Blue House. It is now a museum.

Many of Kahlo's paintings are self-portraits, or paintings she made of herself.

Tour Book

Have you ever been to Mexico? If you visit the country, here are some places to go and things to do!

 Explore

See the Pyramid of Kukulcán at Chichén Itzá. Mayan religious ceremonies took place there. It was also a place for leaders to speak. When you clap, a sound like a birdcall comes back!

Watch

See a bullfight! Modern bullfighting started in the 1700s in Spain. Mexico City has the world's largest bullring. It seats about 55,000 people!

 # Listen

Dance to the sounds of mariachi bands. Sometimes they are seen walking along city streets.

 # Play

Build a sand castle on the beaches of the Maya Riviera. You can also collect seashells and play in waves!

See

Hike in Chipinque Ecological Park near Monterrey. People go there to see birds or bike on trails.

A GREAT COUNTRY

The story of Mexico is important to our world. The people and places that make up this country offer something special. They help make the world a more beautiful, interesting place.

People visit Tulum to see the ruins of an ancient Mayan city.

Mexico Up Close

Official Name: Estados Unidos Mexicanos
(United Mexican States)

Flag:

Population (rank): 114,975,406
(July 2012 est.)
(11th most-populated country)

Total Area (rank): 758,449 square miles
(14th largest country)

Capital: Mexico City

Official Language: Spanish

Currency: Mexican peso

Form of Government: Federal republic

National Anthem: "Himno Nacional de Mexico"
(National Anthem of Mexico)

Important Words

capital a city where government leaders meet.

civilization a well-organized and advanced society.

conquer (KAHN-kuhr) to take control using military force.

federal republic a form of government in which the people choose the leader. The central government and the individual states share power.

metropolitan of or relating to a large city, usually with nearby smaller cities called suburbs.

resource a supply of something useful or valued.

revolution the forced overthrow of a government for a new system.

tradition a belief, a custom, or a story handed down from older people to younger people.

volcano a deep opening in Earth's surface from which hot liquid rock or steam comes out.

Web Sites

To learn more about Mexico, visit ABDO Publishing Company online. Web sites about Mexico are featured on our Book Links page. These links are routinely monitored and updated to provide the most current information available.

www.abdopublishing.com

Index